WH GROWS

A Legacy in Bloom

Bradley Anderson

Copyright © 2024

All Rights Reserved.

No Part of this book may be produced, stored in a retrieval system, or transmitted by any means without the written permission of the author

Dedication

To my late wife

You were my saviour

You were my life

You were my love

You showed me love

You gave my life meaning

I will miss, mourn, and grieve till we meet again.

LOVE YOU

Table of Contents

Dedication ii

Chapter 1 The Diagnosis 1

Chapter 2 The Weight of Decisions 11

Chapter 3 The First Battle 22

Chapter 4 The Struggles of Illness 32

Chapter 5 A New Chapter Begins 43

Chapter 6 The Arrival of Jack and the Strength of Family 52

Chapter 7 The Unseen Battles 62

Chapter 8 The Tides of Change 73

Chapter 9: The Final Goodbye 82

Chapter 10 The Healing Begins 88

Chapter 11 A Legacy of Love 93

Chapter 12 A New Generation 99

Chapter 1
The Diagnosis

The summer of 2014 in Pasadena, Newfoundland, was unusually warm. The sky stretched endlessly; a canvas of bright blue punctuated by the occasional white cloud drifting lazily overhead. Karen's garden was at its peak, bursting with color and life—her pride and joy. Rows of vibrant flowers lined the path to the house, and the strawberry beds, carefully nurtured over the years, were heavy with ripe, red fruit. The pergola, entwined with climbing roses, provided a shaded sanctuary where Karen often sat with a cup of tea, enjoying the fruits of her labor.

Lately, however, even the simple pleasure of tending her garden has become difficult. Karen had always been a woman of energy and resilience. However, over the past few months, she had noticed a persistent fatigue that sapped her strength. The ache in her abdomen had grown more pronounced, and her legs, once so strong and capable, now felt leaden, as if each step required an enormous effort. She had tried to brush it off, attributing it to age or perhaps the demands of maintaining her beloved garden, but deep down, she knew something was wrong.

Bradley had noticed, too. He wasn't one to worry easily, but as the weeks passed, his concern grew. One evening, as they sat together on the porch, the golden light of the setting sun casting long shadows across the lawn, he gently broached the subject.

"Karen, you haven't been yourself lately," Bradley said, his voice tinged with worry. He looked at her with those deep, kind eyes that had always made her feel safe. "You're tired all the time, and I've seen you wince when you think I'm not looking. I think it's time we saw a doctor."

Karen sighed, her gaze drifting to the garden that had brought her so much joy. "I know, Bradley," she admitted softly, a hint of reluctance in her voice. "I've been putting it off, but you're right. Something isn't right. I'll make an appointment tomorrow."

The next day, Karen kept her word. She called Dr. Sullivan, her family physician, in Corner Brook, a town about twenty minutes away. Dr. Sullivan had been their doctor for years — a gentle, attentive man with a calming presence. He had seen her through colds, the flu, and the usual aches and pains that come with age, but this was different. When Karen described her symptoms over the phone, his voice, usually so steady, took on a tone of concern.

"We need to get you in for some tests, Karen," Dr. Sullivan said, his calm demeanor not entirely masking the urgency in his voice. "I'd like you to come in for a full examination and a CT[1] scan as soon as possible."

The appointment was scheduled for the following week. Bradley insisted on coming with her, and Karen was secretly glad for his company. The drive to Corner Brook was quiet, the early morning fog still clinging to the trees along the road. Karen tried to keep her mind occupied by focusing on the familiar landmarks they passed — the small fishing boats bobbing in the harbor, the colorful houses that lined the coast — but her thoughts kept returning to the dull ache in her abdomen and the fatigue that seemed to grow worse by the day.

When they arrived at the clinic, Dr. Sullivan greeted them with his usual warm smile. However, Karen noticed the slight furrow in his brow as he led them into his office. After the

---

[1] Computed Tomography: A CT scan is an imaging test that helps healthcare providers detect diseases and injuries. It uses a series of X-rays and a computer to create detailed images of your bones and soft tissues.

initial examination, he sent Karen for a CT scan, and they were asked to wait in the small, sterile waiting room. The minutes ticked by slowly, each one adding to the knot of anxiety in Karen's stomach.

Finally, Dr. Sullivan called them back into his office. He gestured for them to sit down; his expression serious as he looked over the scan results.

"Karen," he began, his voice gentle but firm, "the CT scan has revealed a mass in your colon. It's quite large, and we need to address it immediately."

Karen felt the world tilt around her — a mass. The word echoed in her mind, heavy and foreboding. She glanced at Bradley, whose hand was suddenly gripping hers tightly, his knuckles white.

"What does that mean?" Bradley asked, his voice steady but laced with concern.

Dr. Sullivan leaned forward, his eyes meeting Karen's. "It means you have colon cancer. Based on the size of the mass and the other symptoms you've described, it's likely Stage III. The cancer has spread beyond the lining of your colon and into nearby lymph nodes, but we haven't found any evidence that it's spread to distant organs."

The room seemed to close in around Karen.

Cancer!

She had heard the word so many times in her life, but it had always been something that happened to other people—something distant and abstract. Now, it was her reality.

"What happens next?" Karen managed to ask, her voice trembling.

"The first step is surgery," Dr. Sullivan explained. "We'll need to remove the tumor along with a portion of your colon—about 13 inches. The procedure is called a partial colectomy. We'll also remove nearby lymph nodes to determine the extent of the cancer's spread. After the surgery, you'll need to undergo chemotherapy to target any remaining cancer cells and reduce the risk of recurrence."

Karen nodded slowly, trying to absorb the flood of information. Surgery. Chemotherapy. It all seemed overwhelming. "What are the chances?" she asked quietly.

Dr. Sullivan paused, choosing his words carefully. "Stage 3 colon cancer is serious, but it's still treatable. The five-year survival rate is around 53% with surgery and chemotherapy. Every case is unique, but we're going to do everything we can to fight this."

Bradley squeezed her hand, his grip firm and reassuring. "We're going to fight this, Karen," he said, his voice filled with determination. "We're going to do whatever it takes."

The drive home was silent, both of them lost in their thoughts. When they arrived back at the house, Karen went straight to the garden, needing the comfort of the familiar sights and smells. She knelt by the strawberry beds, the rich earth cool beneath her hands, and let the tears she had been holding back finally fall.

Later that evening, as they sat together on the porch, Bradley broke the silence. "We need to tell the boys."

Karen nodded, wiping her eyes. "I know. They need to know what's happening."

They decided to call Justin and Greg together, knowing that this news would be hard for them to hear. Justin was the first to pick up, his voice cheerful as he greeted them. But the tone quickly changed as Karen began to explain.

"Mom, are you okay?" Justin asked. His voice was tight with worry.

"I'm going to be, Justin," Karen replied, trying to keep her voice steady. "But I have cancer. Stage III colon cancer. I'm going to need surgery and chemotherapy."

There was a long pause on the other end of the line. When Justin spoke again, his voice was thick with emotion. "Mom, we're going to get through this. Whatever you need, I'm here. We're all here."

Greg's reaction was much the same. He had always been the quieter of the two, more reserved, but Karen could hear the fear in his voice as he tried to process the news.

"Mom, I'm coming home," Greg said. "Sheena and I will drive down tomorrow."

Karen felt a rush of gratitude for her sons and their unwavering support. "You don't have to do that, Greg," she said, though she knew he would come regardless.

"We're family," Greg replied simply. "We'll get through this together."

The next few days passed in a blur of preparations and emotions. Karen and Bradley made arrangements for the surgery, scheduled for the following week in St. John's. They also began to share the news with close friends and extended family, each conversation a painful reminder of the battle that lay ahead.

On the day of the surgery, the hospital in St. John's was bustling with activity. Karen was admitted early in the morning, and the cool air of the hospital was a sharp contrast to the warmth she had left behind in Pasadena. Bradley stayed by her side through the preoperative preparations, holding her hand as the nurses inserted an IV and began to explain what would happen next.

"You'll be under general anesthesia for the surgery," the nurse said, her voice calm and reassuring. "The surgeon will remove the tumor and a portion of your colon. The procedure will take several hours, and you'll be in recovery for a while afterward. Your pain will be managed with medication, and we'll monitor you closely."

Karen nodded, trying to keep her anxiety at bay. "Will it hurt?" she asked, her voice small.

"There will be some discomfort," the nurse admitted, "but we'll make sure you're as comfortable as possible."

Before she knew it, Karen was being wheeled into the operating room. The bright lights overhead were blinding, and the smell of antiseptic filled the air. She felt a rush of fear as the anesthesia began to take effect, her last conscious thought a prayer for strength.

*****

When Karen awoke, the first thing she became aware of was the pain. It was a deep, throbbing ache in her abdomen, spreading outward in waves. Her mouth was dry, and her throat felt raw. She tried to move, but even the slightest shift sent a sharp pain through her body.

"Karen, you're awake," came Bradley's voice, soft and relieved.

She turned her head slowly, seeing him sitting beside her bed, his eyes red-rimmed and tired but full of love. "Bradley," she whispered, her voice hoarse. "It hurts."

"I know," he said gently, reaching out to take

her hand. "The doctor said the surgery went well. They removed the tumor and the affected part of your colon. You're going to be okay, Karen. Just rest."

Karen closed her eyes, focusing on the warmth of Bradley's hand and the sound of his voice. The pain was overwhelming, but so was the sense of relief. The surgery was over, and the first battle was fought and won.

But she knew that this was just the beginning. The road ahead would be long and challenging, filled with more pain, more treatments, and more uncertainty. But as she drifted back to sleep, she clung to the knowledge that she wasn't facing it alone. She had Bradley, Justin, Greg, and their families by her side. And for them, she would keep fighting.

Chapter 2
The Weight of Decisions

The days following Karen's surgery were a blur of pain, recovery, and a profound, bone-weary exhaustion that seemed to permeate every part of her being. The hospital room, with its stark white walls and the constant hum of machines, became both a sanctuary and a prison. Each day was a battle—against the pain, against the fear, and against the overwhelming uncertainty of what the future held.

Karen's body felt foreign to her, a vessel that had been irrevocably altered. The incision on her abdomen, carefully stitched and bandaged, was a constant reminder of the cancer that had invaded her life. The nurses were attentive, administering pain medication, checking her vitals, and encouraging her to take slow, tentative steps around the room to regain her strength. But the slightest movements sent sharp waves of pain through her, and the effort of simply standing left her breathless and weak.

Bradley was by her side through it all. He slept in the uncomfortable hospital chair, his tall frame awkwardly folded into the small space, refusing to leave her alone even for a moment. His eyes, usually so full of warmth and mischief, were shadowed with worry and exhaustion, but he never complained. He held her hand through the worst of the pain, his voice a steady anchor in the storm of her recovery.

"Just breathe, Karen," he would say softly, his hand brushing her hair back from her forehead. "One breath at a time. You're doing great."

Karen clung to his words, drawing strength from his presence. But even with Bradley there, the nights were the hardest. When the hospital quieted down and the darkness settled in, the reality of her situation would crash over her in waves, drowning her in fear and doubt.

One night, unable to sleep, Karen lay in bed, staring up at the ceiling, her thoughts spinning in circles. She could hear the soft beeping of the heart monitor, the occasional murmur of nurses in the hallway, and Bradley's steady breathing beside her. But none of it could quiet the storm raging in her mind.

Where Love Grows

What if the cancer wasn't gone? What if it had spread? What if the chemotherapy didn't work? The questions were relentless, each one feeding her anxiety until it was all she could do to keep from breaking down completely.

The next morning, Dr. Matthews came to see her, his demeanor as calm and professional as ever. He reviewed her charts, asked about her pain levels, and then, finally, delivered the news she had been dreading.

"Karen, we received the pathology report on the lymph nodes we removed during surgery," Dr. Matthews began, his voice steady but serious. "The results show that the cancer has spread to several of the lymph nodes. This means we're dealing with metastatic disease."

Karen felt her stomach drop, the words hitting her like a physical blow. Metastatic. The cancer had spread. She had known this was a possibility, but hearing it confirmed was something else entirely. She felt Bradley's hand tighten around hers, his grip grounding her as the room tangled.

"What does this mean?" Bradley asked, his voice tense.

"It means that we'll need to be aggressive with your treatment," Dr. Matthews replied. "Chemotherapy is the next step. We'll begin with a regimen known as FOLFOX, which includes a combination of three drugs: 5-fluorouracil (5-FU), leucovorin, and oxaliplatin. These drugs work together to target cancer cells and prevent them from growing and dividing."

Karen nodded numbly, the information swirling around her hard to grasp. "How soon can we start?" she asked, her voice small.

"We'll give you a few weeks to recover from the surgery," Dr. Matthews said gently. "We want you to be strong enough to handle the chemotherapy. It's a tough treatment, and it comes with significant side effects. However, it's our best option for targeting the remaining cancer cells."

"What kind of side effects?" Karen asked though part of her didn't want to know.

"Chemotherapy can cause a range of side effects," Dr. Matthews explained. "Nausea and vomiting are common, especially in the first few days after each treatment. We'll prescribe anti-nausea medication to help with that, but it may still be difficult. Fatigue is another major side effect—you'll feel exhausted, and this can last for several days. Hair loss is also possible, as chemotherapy targets all rapidly dividing cells, including hair follicles. There's also the risk of neuropathy, which can cause tingling or numbness in your hands and feet."

Karen swallowed hard, trying to absorb it all. The thought of losing her hair, of her body changing so drastically, filled her with dread. But the fatigue that scared her the most was the idea of being too weak to care for herself, do the things she loved, and be there for her family.

Bradley must have sensed her fear because he leaned closer, his voice firm but gentle. "We'll get through this, Karen. One step at a time. You're not alone in this."

Karen looked at him, her eyes filling with tears. "I'm scared, Bradley," she whispered, her voice trembling. "I'm scared of what this will do to us. To me."

"I know," Bradley said, his voice thick with emotion. "But you're the strongest person I know. We'll face this together, just like we always have."

The days leading up to the start of chemotherapy were a whirlwind of emotions and preparations. Karen was discharged from the hospital, and she and Bradley returned home to Pasadena. The drive back was quiet, both of them lost in their thoughts. The landscape outside the car window passed by in a blur—the familiar roads, the dense forests, and the distant mountains, all seemingly unchanged, even though everything in Karen's world had shifted.

When they arrived home, Karen was greeted by the comforting sight of her garden. The flowers were still in full bloom, the strawberries ripe and ready to be picked. But the garden, once a source of endless joy, now felt like a reminder of everything she might lose.

Justin and Renee were waiting for them at the house, having driven over as soon as they heard about Karen's discharge. The sight of their son and daughter-in-law filled Karen with a mixture of relief and sadness—relief because she knew they were there to support her and sadness because she hated the idea of them seeing her like this, so weak and vulnerable.

"Mom," Justin said as he enveloped her in a gentle hug. "It's so good to have you home."

"Thank you, Justin," Karen said, her voice thick with emotion. "I'm glad to be home."

Renee stepped forward, her eyes filled with concern and love. "We've been thinking about you every day, Karen. We're here for whatever you need."

Karen smiled weakly, her heart swelling with gratitude for her family. "Thank you, Renee. It means so much to me to have you both here."

The four of them spent the afternoon together, sitting in the living room, the conversation light but tinged with the underlying tension of what lay ahead. Karen could feel the weight of their concern, but she also felt the warmth of their love, a reminder that she wasn't facing this battle alone.

Later that evening, after Justin and Renee had gone home, Karen and Bradley sat together on the porch, watching the sun set over the garden. The sky was painted in shades of pink and orange, the air cool and crisp as the day gave way to night.

"Do you think I'm strong enough for this?" Karen asked quietly, her eyes fixed on the horizon.

Bradley turned to look at her, his expression serious but full of love. "I know you are," he said firmly. "You've faced every challenge life has thrown at you with grace and strength. This won't be any different."

Karen sighed, leaning into him, taking comfort in his unwavering support. "I just don't want to be a burden," she whispered. "I don't want this to take away our happiness."

"You're not a burden," Bradley said softly, wrapping his arm around her shoulders. "You never could be. We'll get through this together, one day at a time."

As the days passed, Karen tried to focus on the positives—the fact that the surgery had been successful in removing the tumor, the support of her family, and the strength she drew from Bradley's unwavering presence. But there was no escaping the looming reality of chemotherapy, the next battle in her fight against cancer.

One evening, as they were preparing for bed, Bradley gently broached the subject of telling Greg. Karen had been avoiding the conversation, not wanting to worry about her younger son. However, she knew Bradley was right—it was time to let Greg and Sheena know the full extent of her condition.

"I'll call him tomorrow," Karen said, her voice heavy with resignation. "He deserves to know."

The next day, Karen made the call. Greg answered on the second ring, his voice warm and full of energy. "Hey, Mom! How are you feeling?"

Karen took a deep breath, trying to steady her nerves. "Greg, there's something I need to tell you," She began, her voice trembling slightly. "The surgery went well, but... the cancer has spread to my lymph nodes. I'm going to need chemotherapy."

There was a long pause on the other end of the line, and when Greg spoke again, his voice was quiet, almost hesitant. "How bad is it?"

Where Love Grows

Karen closed her eyes, the words catching in her throat. "It's serious, Greg," she admitted. "But Dr. Matthews is hopeful. We're going to fight this with everything we've got."

"We're coming down," Greg said firmly. "Sheena and

I will be there as soon as we can."

"Greg, you don't have to—" Karen began, but Greg cut her off.

"We're coming, Mom," he repeated, his voice brooking no argument. "You're not going through this alone."

Karen felt a swell of emotion, a mixture of love and guilt. She hated the thought of her illness disrupting their lives, but she also knew she couldn't face this battle without them. "Okay," she said softly. "Thank you, Greg."

When she hung up the phone, Karen felt a strange sense of relief. The news was out, the truth laid bare, and now they could move forward—together.

The following week, Greg and Sheena arrived, their presence a balm to Karen's anxious heart. Sheena, with her warm smile and comforting demeanor, immediately set about helping around the house, preparing meals, and keeping Karen company during the long, quiet hours when Bradley was at work.

Greg, though calmer, offered his support in his own way, sitting with Karen in the garden, talking about everything and nothing, providing a sense of normalcy in the midst of chaos.

As the date for her first chemotherapy treatment approached, Karen found herself oscillating between fear and determination. She knew the road ahead would be difficult, but she also knew she had no choice but to walk it.

One evening, as she and Bradley sat together on the porch, Karen voiced the question that had been haunting her.

"What if it doesn't work, Bradley?" she asked, her voice barely above a whisper. "What if the chemotherapy doesn't stop the cancer?"

Bradley was silent for a moment, his gaze fixed on the horizon. When he finally spoke, his voice was steady and full of resolve. "Then we keep fighting," he simply said. "No matter what happens, we keep fighting. Together."

Karen nodded, feeling a surge of determination. She had faced brutal battles before, but this one was different—this one was for her life, for her future, for the chance to be there for her family.

As the sun dipped below the horizon, casting the garden in a warm, golden glow, Karen made a promise to herself: she would fight with everything she had. For Bradley, for Justin and Greg, for Renee and Sheena, and for the future, she still believed it was possible.

The weight of the decisions before her was heavy, but she knew she wasn't carrying it alone. As she sat there, surrounded by the love and support of her family, Karen found a glimmer of hope in the darkness.

Chapter 3
The First Battle

The weeks leading up to Karen's first chemotherapy session were filled with a strange mix of normalcy and anticipation. The summer days in Pasadena stretched long and warm, and the garden continued to bloom as if nothing had changed. But for Karen, everything had changed. Every flower she tended, every meal she cooked, and every quiet moment she spent with Bradley was tinged with the knowledge of what was to come.

The night before her first treatment, Karen sat at the kitchen table, staring at the calendar. The date of her chemotherapy session was circled in red, a stark reminder of the battle that awaited her. She felt a knot of anxiety tightening in her chest, her mind racing with thoughts of what the next day would bring.

Bradley entered the kitchen, his presence as comforting as ever. He placed a cup of tea in front of her and took a seat across the table, his eyes filled with concern.

"How are you feeling?" he asked gently, his voice breaking the silence.

Karen sighed, wrapping her hands around the warm cup. "I'm scared, Bradley," she admitted, her voice trembling slightly. "I don't know what to expect. I've read about the side effects, but… I'm not ready for this."

Bradley reached across the table, taking her hand in his. "You don't have to be ready, Karen," he said softly. "You just have to take it one step at a time. We'll face it together."

Karen nodded, feeling a lump form in her throat. She was grateful for Bradley's unwavering support, but the fear still gnawed at her. "I don't want you to see me like this," she whispered. "I don't want you to see me weak and sick."

"Karen," Bradley said, his voice firm but filled with love, "I love you. Nothing will change that. We've been through so much together, and we'll get through this too. You don't have to hide how you're feeling from me."

Karen looked into his eyes, seeing the depth of his love and commitment. It gave her the strength she needed to face what was coming. "I'm lucky to have you," she said quietly, squeezing his hand.

"We're lucky to have each other," Bradley replied with a gentle smile.

The following day, Karen woke early, the anxiety from the night before still lingering. She showered and dressed carefully, choosing a soft, comfortable sweater and jeans. She looked at herself in the mirror, trying to find the strength in her reflection. Her hair, still thick and dark, hung around her shoulders, but she knew it wouldn't be long before the chemotherapy would take that from her, too.

When she emerged from the bedroom, Bradley was waiting for her with a small bag packed with essentials—water, snacks, and a book to read during the treatment. He had thought of everything, as usual.

"Ready?" he asked, his voice steady.

Karen took a deep breath and nodded. "As ready as I'll ever be."

The drive to the hospital in Corner Brook was quiet, and both of them were lost in their thoughts. The sun was just beginning to rise, casting a soft, golden light over the landscape. The beauty of the morning felt at odds with the dread weighing heavily on Karen's heart.

When they arrived at the hospital, they were directed to the oncology department. The waiting room was filled with patients in various stages of treatment—some with IVs already hooked up, others waiting for their turn. The air was thick with the sterile scent of antiseptic, and the soft hum of medical equipment provided a constant backdrop.

Karen checked in at the front desk, and the receptionist offered a sympathetic smile as she handed over the necessary paperwork. "You'll be in Room 3, Mrs. Williams. The nurse will be with you shortly."

Bradley held Karen's hand as they made their way to the small, private room. The walls were painted a soothing pale blue, and a comfortable recliner sat in the center, surrounded by medical equipment. Karen took a seat, feeling the cold leather against her skin, and tried to steady her nerves.

A few minutes later, a nurse entered the room, her expression warm and reassuring. "Good morning, Mrs. Williams. My name is Sarah, and I'll be taking care of you today."

Karen forced a smile, grateful for the nurse's kindness. "Thank you," she said, her voice tight with anxiety.

Sarah went through the details of the treatment, explaining each step in a calm, steady voice. "We'll start by administering a combination of three drugs: 5-fluorouracil, leucovorin, and oxaliplatin. These will be delivered through an IV, and the entire process will take about two hours. You might feel some discomfort, but we'll monitor you closely and adjust as needed."

Karen nodded, trying to focus on the information and not the fear that was threatening to overwhelm her. "What kind of discomfort?" she asked, her voice wavering.

"Some patients experience a cold sensation or tingling in their hands and feet, especially with the oxaliplatin," Sarah explained. "You might also feel nauseous or lightheaded. We have medication to help with the nausea, and I'll be here to make sure you're comfortable throughout the treatment."

"Thank you," Karen said quietly, her hands trembling slightly as she gripped the armrests of the recliner.

Sarah moved efficiently, preparing the IV and adjusting the chair so Karen could recline comfortably. Bradley sat beside her, his presence a steady source of comfort. As the IV was inserted into her arm, Karen felt a small prick, followed by a cold sensation spreading through her veins.

"Just breathe, Karen," Bradley whispered, his hand resting gently on her knee. "You're doing great."

Karen closed her eyes, focusing on the sound of Bradley's voice and the rhythm of her own breathing. The room was quiet, with only the soft hum of the IV pump and the occasional rustle of paper as Sarah recorded Karen's vitals.

The first half-hour passed slowly, the cold sensation in Karen's arm growing more intense. She felt a wave of nausea wash over her, and her head began to spin. Sarah was quick to administer anti-nausea medication, which helped ease the discomfort, but the overall experience was far from pleasant.

As the treatment progressed, Karen's thoughts drifted to her family. She wondered how Justin and Greg were handling the news, whether they were as scared as she was. She thought about Lucy, who would be born in just a few short years, and the other grandchildren who would follow. She had to fight for them, for the chance to be a part of their lives.

Bradley stayed by her side the entire time, his presence a constant reassurance. He held her hand when nausea became overwhelming, and he read to her from the book they had brought when the treatment dragged on, and she needed a distraction.

Finally, after what felt like an eternity, Sarah returned to the room to remove the IV. "You did great, Mrs. Williams," she said with a smile. "The first treatment is always the hardest, but you got through it."

Karen nodded, too exhausted to respond. She felt drained, both physically and emotionally, the weight of the treatment settling over her like a heavy blanket.

"How do you feel?" Bradley asked, his voice soft and concerned.

"Tired," Karen whispered, her eyelids heavy. "So tired."

Bradley helped her to her feet, his arm around her waist as they slowly made their way out of the hospital. The walk to the car seemed longer than usual, each step an effort. By the time they reached the car, Karen felt as though she had run a marathon.

The drive home was quiet, Karen leaning back in her seat, her eyes closed as she tried to block out the nausea and fatigue. Bradley reached over occasionally to squeeze her hand, his silent support a comfort in the overwhelming silence.

Where Love Grows

When they arrived home, Bradley helped Karen inside and into bed. The moment her head hit the pillow, the exhaustion took over, pulling her into a deep, dreamless sleep.

*****

The days following the treatment were some of the hardest Karen had ever faced. The nausea lingered, making it difficult to eat, and the fatigue was unlike anything she had ever experienced. It was a bone-deep exhaustion that no amount of rest could alleviate, leaving her feeling weak and helpless.

Bradley was a constant presence, caring for her with a tenderness that brought tears to her eyes. He made sure she drank plenty of water, got her small, simple meals that she could manage, and sat with her during the long hours when nausea and fatigue made it impossible to do anything but lie in bed.

"You're doing great, Karen," he would say, his voice filled with quiet encouragement. "Just take it one day at a time."

Karen tried to focus on the positives — the fact that the treatment was targeting the cancer that she was fighting back. But there were moments when the fear and pain became too much, and she found herself questioning whether she could continue.

One afternoon, as Karen lay in bed, the curtains drawn against the bright summer sun, she felt a wave of despair wash over her. The thought of facing another round of chemotherapy, of enduring this pain and exhaustion again and again, was almost too much to bear.

"I don't know if I can do this, Bradley," she whispered, her voice trembling with emotion. "I don't know if I'm strong enough."

Bradley sat beside her on the bed, his hand gently stroking her hair. "You are strong, Karen," he said softly. "Stronger than you know. And you don't have to do this alone. I'm here with you every step of the way."

Karen closed her eyes, the tears slipping down her cheeks. "I'm so scared," she admitted, her voice barely above a whisper. "I'm scared of what this will do to me, to us."

Bradley leaned down, pressing a kiss to her forehead. "We'll get through this, Karen," he said, his voice filled with quiet conviction. "Together. We'll take it one day at a time and get through it."

Karen nodded, trying to draw strength from his words. She knew that the road ahead would be long and complex, but she also knew she had no choice but to keep fighting. For Bradley, for

Justin and Greg, and for the future, she still hoped to be a part of it.

As the days passed, Karen slowly began to regain some of her strength. The nausea subsided, and the fatigue, while still present, became more manageable. She found solace in the small things—sitting in the garden for a few minutes each day, reading a book, or simply holding Bradley's hand.

The first battle had been fought, and though Karen knew there were many more to come, she felt a flicker of hope. She had made it through the first treatment, and with the love and support of her family, she would face whatever came next.

Chapter 4
The Struggles of Illness

The weeks that followed Karen's first chemotherapy session were a test of her strength and resolve. Each treatment seemed to bring new challenges, both physically and emotionally, and as summer faded into autumn, Karen found herself grappling with the harsh realities of her illness in ways she hadn't anticipated.

Chemotherapy became a routine, one that Karen dreaded but endured. Every two weeks, she and Bradley would make the trip to the hospital in Corner Brook, the drive familiar yet heavy with the weight of what awaited her. The treatments were grueling—each session left her more drained than the last, the nausea and fatigue a constant presence in her life. The anti-nausea medications helped, but there were days when even the thought of food made her stomach churn.

Where Love Grows

The side effects were relentless. The cold sensitivity from the oxaliplatin made even the simplest tasks—like drinking a glass of water or reaching into the refrigerator—painful. The tingling and numbness in her hands and feet, a symptom of neuropathy, made it difficult to hold objects or even walk without stumbling. But it was the fatigue that weighed on her the most. It was a bone-deep exhaustion that no amount of rest could alleviate, leaving her feeling weak, frail, and disconnected from the life she had once known.

As the treatments progressed, Karen began to notice other changes as well. Her hair, once thick and dark, started to thin. At first, it was just a few strands on her pillow in the morning or a small clump in the shower drain. But soon, it became impossible to ignore. Every time she ran her fingers through her hair, more would come out until she was left with handfuls of it. It was a painful, heartbreaking process, one that stripped away not just her hair but a piece of her identity.

One morning, as Karen stood in front of the bathroom mirror, she stared at her reflection, her hands trembling as she touched the thinning patches on her scalp. She had always taken pride in her appearance—her hair had been one of her favorite features. Now, it was disappearing, just another casualty in the war her body was waging against itself.

She felt a wave of despair wash over her, a deep, aching sadness that made her want to collapse on the bathroom floor and cry until there were no tears left. But she didn't. Instead, she reached for the scissors on the counter, her hands shaking as she made the decision to take control of something in her life, something that seemed so utterly out of her hands.

Bradley found her there, standing in front of the mirror with the scissors poised over her hair. He entered the bathroom quietly, his heart breaking at the sight of her. Without saying a word, he took the scissors from her hand and gently guided her to a chair.

"Let me help," he said softly, his voice thick with emotion.

Karen nodded, unable to speak past the lump in her throat. She sat down, and Bradley began to carefully cut what was left of her hair. Each snip of the scissors felt like a dagger to his heart, but he kept his hands steady, determined to do this for her, to ease the pain in any way he could.

When he was done, Karen looked at herself in the mirror, her scalp now mostly bare, with only a few patches of hair remaining. She felt exposed, vulnerable, and yet, in some small way, liberated.

This was one more thing the cancer had taken from her, but it was also something she had chosen to let go of on her own terms.

Bradley wrapped his arms around her from behind, resting his chin on her shoulder. "You're beautiful, Karen," he whispered, his voice full of love and sincerity. "Hair or no hair, you're still the most beautiful woman I've ever known."

Karen closed her eyes, leaning into him, letting his words wash over her. She knew he meant it, but it didn't make the loss any easier to bear. Still, she was grateful for his unwavering support, his ability to see beyond the physical changes and his love that remained steadfast, even in the face of everything they were going through.

The physical changes were only part of the struggle. Emotionally, Karen found herself on an exhausting roller coaster, her moods swinging from hope to despair, often within the same day. The steroids that she was taking to help with the side effects of chemotherapy added to the volatility, making her feel irritable and restless.

There were days when she would snap at Bradley or the boys for no reason, the frustration and anger bubbling over before she could stop it.

But it was the moments of deep sadness that were the hardest. There were times when Karen felt like she was drowning in a sea of grief—grieving for the life she had before cancer, for the things she was losing, and for the uncertainty of what lay ahead. She missed the person she used to be, the woman who could spend hours in the garden, who laughed easily and without fear, who didn't have to worry about whether she would be around to see her grandchildren grow up.

One evening, as she sat on the porch with Bradley, watching the sun set over the garden, Karen broke down. The weight of everything she had been holding in finally became too much, and she dissolved into tears, her body shaking with sobs.

Bradley pulled her into his arms, holding her tightly as she cried, his own eyes wet with unshed tears. "It's okay, Karen," he whispered, his voice breaking. "It's okay to let it out. I'm here. I've got you."

"I'm exhausted, Bradley," Karen sobbed, her voice muffled against his chest. "I'm so tired of being strong. I don't know if I can do this anymore."

"You don't have to be strong all the time," Bradley said gently, his hand stroking her back. "You're allowed to feel tired, to feel sad. But

Where Love Grows

you're not alone in this. We'll get through it together."

Karen clung to him, feeling both comforted and exhausted. The tears eventually subsided, leaving her feeling drained but lighter, as if a small part of the burden had been lifted.

"I'm scared," she admitted quietly, her voice barely above a whisper. "I'm scared of what this is doing to us, to me."

"I know," Bradley said softly, his heart aching at the vulnerability in her voice. "But no matter what, I'm not going anywhere. We're in this together, Karen. Always."

As the weeks turned into months, Karen and Bradley settled into a new routine — one dictated by the cycles of chemotherapy, the days of recovery, and the small pockets of normalcy they tried to hold onto. The garden became a refuge for Karen, even though she could no longer tend to it as she once did. She would sit on the porch, wrapped in a blanket, and watch as the flowers bloomed and the leaves changed colors with the seasons. It was a reminder that life continued, even in the midst of illness, and that there was still beauty to be found, even in the hardest of times.

The support from their family was unwavering. Justin and Renee visited often, bringing meals and helping with household chores. They spent hours sitting with Karen, talking, laughing, and sometimes just being there, offering the kind of comfort that only family could provide. Greg and Sheena made the long drive from St. John's whenever they could, their presence a balm to Karen's weary soul.

One challenging day, as Karen was recovering from another round of chemotherapy, she received a call from Greg. His voice was filled with excitement, a welcome contrast to the heaviness that had settled over her.

"Mom, I have some news," Greg said, barely able to contain his enthusiasm.

"What is it, Greg?" Karen asked, her interest piqued despite her exhaustion.

"Sheena and I are expecting," Greg announced, his voice brimming with joy. "You're going to be a grandmother again!"

Karen felt a surge of emotion, a mix of joy, relief, and hope. "Oh, Greg, that's wonderful news!" she exclaimed, tears filling her eyes. "When is the baby due?"

"Early next year," Greg replied. "We wanted you to be the first to know."

Where Love Grows

Karen smiled, her heart swelling with happiness. "Thank you, Greg. This is the best news I've heard in a long time."

The news of another grandchild brought a renewed sense of purpose to Karen's life. She had something to look forward to, something to fight for. The thought of holding her new grandchild, of watching them grow up, filled her with a determination she hadn't felt in months.

As the holidays approached, Karen's spirits lifted. Christmas had always been her favorite time of year—a season of warmth, family, and tradition. Despite her illness, she was determined to make it a special time for everyone. With Bradley's help, she began planning the holiday gatherings, deciding on the menu, decorating the house, and, of course, baking.

Baking had always been one of Karen's greatest joys, and it was a tradition she was determined to keep alive, even if it meant enlisting help from her family. She spent hours in the kitchen with Renee, teaching her the recipes that had been passed down through generations—the perfect shortbread cookies, the rich, buttery fruitcake, and the chocolate yule log that had always been a family favorite.

"Renee, you're a natural," Karen said one afternoon as they worked together in the kitchen, the sweet smell of baking filling the air. "I'm so glad we're doing this together."

"I'm just glad I can help," Renee replied with a smile, her hands covered in flour as she rolled out the dough. "This means a lot to me, Karen. I love learning from you."

Karen felt a warmth in her chest, a sense of continuity that transcended her illness. "It's important to me that these traditions live on," she said softly. "Even when I'm not here, I want you all to have these memories, these recipes."

Renee paused, looking at Karen with a mixture of love and sadness. "You're going to be here, Karen," she said firmly. "We're going to make sure of it."

Karen smiled, though a part of her knew that no one could make such promises. But for now, she was content to focus on the present, on the joy of baking with her family, and on the love that surrounded her.

The holidays were a time of celebration, a brief respite from the harsh realities of cancer. The house was filled with laughter, the sounds of children playing, and the smell of delicious food. Karen watched as her family gathered around the table, her heart full as she saw the joy in their faces.

Where Love Grows

As they sat down to Christmas dinner, the table laden with all of Karen's favorite dishes, Bradley raised his glass in a toast.

"To Karen," he said, his voice thick with emotion. "For making this Christmas so special, for being the heart of our family, and for showing us all what true strength and love look like."

The family raised their glasses, their eyes shining with love and admiration for the woman who had brought them all together. Karen smiled, her eyes wet with tears, feeling a deep sense of gratitude for the love that surrounded her.

The months that followed were filled with ups and downs — moments of joy and hope tempered by the relentless challenges of illness. But through it all, Karen held onto the knowledge that she was not alone. She had her family, her garden, and the traditions that had carried them through so many seasons of life.

And as winter turned to spring, Karen found herself looking forward to the future with a quiet determination. There were more battles to be fought and more challenges to face, but she knew she would face them with the same strength and grace that had carried her this far.

Because no matter how arduous the journey was, Karen knew that love would always be more robust than illness and that the memories they were creating together would endure long after the pain had faded away.

Chapter 5
A New Chapter Begins

As spring arrived in 2017, Karen felt a renewed sense of hope. The harsh winter had finally given way to warmer days, and with the change in seasons came a shift in Karen's outlook. The news that she was going to be a grandmother again — twice over, with both Renee and Sheena expecting — brought a joy that brightened even the darkest moments of her battle with cancer.

Karen's health had stabilized somewhat after the initial rounds of chemotherapy. The side effects were still there, but she had learned to manage them better, finding ways to navigate the nausea, fatigue, and neuropathy that had become part of her daily life. Her hair had begun to grow back, though it was thinner and lighter than before, and she had grown accustomed to the sight of her new reflection in the mirror.

But it was the anticipation of the new lives soon to join the family that gave Karen the most strength. She spent hours dreaming about the future — about the days she would spend with her grandchildren, teaching them to bake, showing them the wonders of her garden, and creating new memories that would carry her legacy forward.

By late June, as Renee's due date approached, Karen could hardly contain her excitement. She had prepared everything for Lucy's arrival, even setting up a small nursery in the guest room for when Renee and Justin brought the baby to visit. The crib was freshly made with soft, pink linens, and a collection of carefully chosen baby clothes hung neatly in the closet. Karen had even knitted a tiny sweater and matching booties, each stitch a labor of love.

On July 15, 2017, the long-awaited day finally arrived. Karen and Bradley were at home when they received the call from Justin. The moment Karen heard her son's voice on the other end of the line, she knew.

"Mom, she's here," Justin said, his voice thick with emotion. "Lucy's here, and she's perfect."

Karen felt a rush of joy and relief, tears springing to her eyes. "Oh, Justin, I'm so happy for you and Renee," she said, her voice trembling. "How's Renee? How's the baby?"

Where Love Grows

"They're both doing great," Justin replied, his voice filled with pride. "Lucy's healthy, and Renee is resting now. We can't wait for you to meet her."

Karen's heart swelled with love for her new granddaughter, and she could hardly wait to hold Lucy in her arms. "We'll be there as soon as we can," she promised. "Give Renee a kiss for me, and tell her how proud I am of her."

As soon as the call ended, Karen turned to Bradley, her eyes shining with excitement. "We're grandparents again," she said, a broad smile spreading across her face.

Bradley grinned, pulling her into a hug. "I can't wait to meet her," he said, his voice filled with warmth. "You're going to be the best Nanny Ner, Karen."

The next day, Karen and Bradley made the drive to St. John's to meet their new granddaughter. The eight-hour journey was filled with anticipation, the miles passing slowly as they neared the city. Karen's thoughts were consumed with the idea of Lucy—wondering what she would look like, how it would feel to finally hold her, and all the dreams she had for the little girl's future.

When they arrived at the hospital, Karen's heart raced with excitement. They made their way to the maternity ward, where Justin was waiting for them in the hallway, a broad smile on his face.

"Mom, Dad, come meet your granddaughter," Justin said, his voice brimming with pride.

Karen's breath caught in her throat as they entered the room. There, in Renee's arms, was the most beautiful baby girl Karen had ever seen. Lucy was wrapped in a soft pink blanket, her tiny face peeking out, her eyes closed as she slept peacefully.

"Oh, Justin... she's perfect," Karen whispered, tears streaming down her face as she approached the bed.

Renee smiled, her own eyes filled with love and exhaustion. "Would you like to hold her, Karen?" she asked softly.

Karen nodded, her hands trembling with emotion as she gently took Lucy into her arms. The moment she held her granddaughter, Karen felt a deep, overwhelming love that filled every part of her being. Lucy was so small, so delicate, her tiny fingers curling around Karen's as she stirred in her sleep.

"Welcome to the world, Lucy," Karen whispered, pressing a gentle kiss to the baby's forehead. "I'm your Nanny Ner, and I'm going to love you so much."

Bradley stood beside her, his eyes moist with emotion as he looked down at his granddaughter. "She's beautiful, Karen," he said quietly, his voice full of awe. "Just like her grandmother."

Karen smiled through her tears, her heart full to bursting with love and gratitude. This moment, this precious gift of new life, was everything she had fought for, everything she had dreamed of. And as she held Lucy close, she knew that no matter what challenges lay ahead, this was worth it.

The days that followed were filled with joy and celebration. Karen and Bradley stayed with Justin and Renee for a few days, helping with the baby and soaking in every moment with their new granddaughter. Karen cherished every smile, every tiny movement, every sound Lucy made. She sang to her, rocked her to sleep, and told her stories about the garden they would explore together when she was older.

But amid the joy, Karen also felt a sense of urgency. She knew that time was precious and that the future was uncertain. She wanted to make the most of every moment, to create as many memories as possible with Lucy and the rest of her family.

When they returned to Pasadena, Karen threw herself into her garden work with renewed vigor. The anticipation of Jack's arrival in December, followed by Anna's in August 2020, gave her a sense of purpose that drove her forward. She began planning for the future—designing a particular section of the garden just for the grandchildren, where they could play and explore, surrounded by the beauty she had cultivated over the years.

As the months passed, Karen found herself reflecting on the journey she had been on. Cancer, the treatments, the pain—it had all been overwhelming at times, but it had also brought her closer to her family, deepened her appreciation for the simple joys of life, and strengthened her resolve to fight for the future.

One afternoon, as Karen sat on the porch, looking out over the garden, she found herself thinking about her father. He had always been a strong presence in her life, a man who had faced his own battle with cancer with quiet dignity and strength. She remembered how he used to sit with her in the garden, telling her stories and teaching her about the plants they tended together. It was his love of gardening that had inspired her own, and now, as she faced her own challenges, she felt a deep connection to him.

Where Love Grows

"I wish you were here, Dad," Karen whispered, her eyes filling with tears. "I wish you could meet your great-granddaughter and see the garden I've made. I miss you so much."

As she sat there, lost in her memories, Karen felt a sense of peace wash over her. She knew her father was with her in spirit, guiding her and giving her the strength to keep going. And she knew that as long as she had her family, as long as she had her garden, she would always have something to fight for.

The months flew by, and before Karen knew it, December had arrived. The holiday season was always a special time for the Williams family, and this year was no exception. With Jack's arrival just around the corner, the anticipation of another grandchild added an extra layer of excitement to the festivities.

Karen, despite the fatigue and lingering effects of chemotherapy, was determined to make this Christmas one to remember. She spent hours in the kitchen baking cookies, pies, and the traditional fruitcake that had been a staple at every Williams family Christmas for generations. Bradley helped her with the heavier tasks, chopping firewood and hanging decorations, while Karen focused on the details that made the holidays feel magical.

The house was soon filled with the smells of baking, the sound of Christmas music, and the laughter of family gathered together. Justin, Renee, and baby Lucy arrived a few days before Christmas, their presence filling the house with joy. Greg and Sheena, now heavily pregnant, made the long drive from St. John's, their arrival greeted with hugs and excitement.

On Christmas Eve, after the meal had been enjoyed and the dishes cleared away, the family gathered around the fireplace, the glow of the fire casting a warm light over the room. Karen sat with Lucy in her lap, the baby's soft coos and giggles bringing a smile to everyone's face.

As the night drew to a close, Bradley stood and raised his glass. "To the family," he said, his voice thick with emotion. "To the love that binds us together, through good times and bad. And to Karen, who is the heart of this family, the one who makes every moment special."

Karen's eyes filled with tears as she looked around at her family, her heart swelling with love and gratitude. "I love you all so much," she said, her voice trembling. "Thank you for being my strength, for giving me so much to fight for."

As they clinked their glasses and drank to the toast, Karen felt a deep sense of contentment. This was what she had fought for — the love, the laughter, the memories. And as she looked down at Lucy, now fast asleep in her arms, she knew that no matter what the future held, she would face it with courage and love.

Chapter 6
The Arrival of Jack and the Strength of Family

The months following Lucy's birth were a period of immense joy and anticipation for Karen. The summer of 2017 had been marked by the sweet presence of her first granddaughter, and now, as the year neared its end, Karen's thoughts were consumed with the arrival of her next grandchild — Greg and Sheena's baby, who was due in December.

Karen's health remained stable throughout the latter half of the year despite the ongoing effects of chemotherapy. The treatments were still grueling, but she had adapted to the routine, finding ways to cope with the fatigue and other side effects. Bradley remained her constant support, always by her side, offering quiet encouragement and practical help. They had settled into a rhythm, one that balanced the demands of her illness with the joy of their growing family.

As December approached, the weather turned colder, and the first snowfall of the season blanketed Pasadena in a layer of pristine white. The garden, now dormant under the snow, stood as a reminder of the cycle of life—of growth, rest, and renewal. Karen often found herself gazing out at the snow-covered landscape, her thoughts drifting to the new life that was soon to enter the world.

Greg and Sheena decided to stay in St. John's for the birth, given the proximity to the hospital and their doctor. Karen understood the practicalities, but she couldn't help feeling a pang of sadness that she wouldn't be there for the birth itself. However, she and Bradley had made plans to visit as soon as possible after the baby was born.

On the morning of December 12, 2017, Karen's phone rang, the familiar ringtone of Greg's number bringing a smile to her face. She answered quickly, her heart racing with excitement.

"Mom, he's here!" Greg's voice was filled with joy and exhaustion. "Jack is here, and he's perfect."

Karen felt a rush of emotion, tears springing to her eyes. "Oh, Greg, I'm so happy for you and Sheena," she said, her voice trembling. "How is she? How is Jack?"

"Sheena's doing great," Greg replied, his voice brimming with pride. "Jack's healthy, and he's got a good set of lungs on him. We can't wait for you to meet him."

Karen's heart swelled with love for her new grandson. "We'll be there as soon as we can," she promised. "Give Sheena a kiss for me, and tell her how proud I am of her."

As soon as the call ended, Karen turned to Bradley, who was watching her with a knowing smile. "We're grandparents again," she said, her voice full of emotion.

Bradley grinned, pulling her into a hug. "That's wonderful news, Karen. I can't wait to meet him."

The following day, Karen and Bradley packed their bags and set out for St. John's. The eight-hour drive, which had become so familiar over the years, felt different this time—filled with anticipation and joy. Karen's thoughts were consumed with the idea of meeting Jack, of holding him in her arms and seeing Greg and Sheena as parents for the first time.

When they arrived at the hospital, the excitement in the air was palpable. Greg met them in the hallway, his face lit up with a smile that Karen hadn't seen in years. He led them to

Where Love Grows

Sheena's room, where the new family of three was waiting.

Sheena was sitting up in bed, looking tired but radiant, with a small bundle cradled in her arms. As Karen and Bradley entered the room, Sheena's face broke into a warm smile.

"Karen, Bradley, meet Jack," she said softly, lifting the blanket slightly so they could see the tiny face beneath.

Karen's breath caught in her throat as she looked down at her grandson. Jack was perfect—tiny, with dark hair and rosy cheeks, his eyes closed as he slept peacefully. Karen felt a wave of love and gratitude wash over her, and she reached out to take him into her arms.

"Welcome to the world, Jack," Karen whispered, her voice thick with emotion. "I'm your Nanny Ner, and I'm going to love you so much."

Bradley stood beside her, his eyes moist with emotion as he looked down at his grandson. "He's beautiful, Karen," he said quietly, his voice filled with awe. "Just like Lucy."

Karen smiled through her tears, feeling a deep sense of contentment. This moment, this precious gift of new life, was everything she had hoped for, everything she had fought for. And as she held

Jack close, she knew it was worth it no matter what challenges lay ahead.

The next few days were a blur of joy and celebration. Karen and Bradley stayed with Greg and Sheena, helping with the baby and soaking in every moment with their new grandson. Karen cherished every smile, every tiny movement, every sound Jack made. She sang to him, rocked him to sleep, and told him stories about the garden and the adventures they would have together.

But amid the joy, Karen also felt a deep sense of responsibility. She wanted to create memories for Jack, just as she had for Lucy — memories that would last a lifetime. She spent hours talking with Greg and Sheena about their hopes and dreams for Jack, the values they wanted to instill in him, and the legacy she hoped to leave behind.

One evening, as Karen sat in the nursery with Jack in her arms, Greg joined her, a thoughtful expression on his face.

"Mom," Greg began, his voice quiet, "I've been thinking a lot about the future, about what kind of father I want to be. And I keep coming back to you and Dad. You've always been there for us, no matter what. I want to be that kind of parent for Jack."

Karen smiled, her heart swelling with pride. "You're already an amazing father, Greg," she said softly. "And you'll continue to be because you have so much love to give. Just remember that it's okay to ask for help and lean on family. We're all in this together."

Greg nodded, his eyes filled with gratitude. "Thank you, Mom. That means a lot. I want Jack to know the same kind of love and support that Justin and I have always felt from you."

"He will, Greg," Karen assured him. "Because you and Sheena will show him that love every day. And we'll be here to help every step of the way."

As they sat together in the quiet of the nursery, Karen felt a deep sense of peace. Her family was growing, and with it, the love and connections that had always been the foundation of her life. The challenges of her illness were still present, but in these moments, they felt distant, overshadowed by the joy and hope that surrounded her.

The holidays that year were especially meaningful. With Jack's arrival just before Christmas, the Williams family had even more reason to celebrate. The house was filled with laughter, the sounds of children playing, and the warmth of family gathered together. Karen, despite her ongoing battle with cancer, was determined to make this Christmas as special as possible.

She decorated the house carefully, baking her favorite holiday treats and ensuring the traditions she cherished were upheld. Every moment felt precious, and Karen embraced the season with a whole heart, knowing that it wasn't just about celebrating the holiday but also creating memories that her family would hold onto for years to come.

She spent hours in the kitchen with Renee, baking cookies and preparing the holiday feast. The two of them worked side by side, sharing stories and laughter as they prepared the dishes that had become a staple of the Williams family Christmas. Karen was particularly excited to introduce Jack to the holiday traditions, even if he was too young to understand them fully.

"Next year, Jack will be running around with Lucy, getting into everything," Karen said with a smile as she placed a tray of cookies in the oven. "But this year, we'll just enjoy the quiet moments."

Renee nodded; her hands busy decorating a batch of sugar cookies. "I'm so glad we can do this

Where Love Grows

together, Karen. These are the moments that matter."

Karen felt a warmth in her chest, a sense of continuity that transcended her illness. "It's important to me that these traditions live on," she said softly. "Even when I'm not here, I want you all to have these memories, these recipes."

Renee paused, looking at Karen with a mixture of love and sadness. "You're going to be here, Karen," she said firmly. "We're going to make sure of it."

Karen smiled, though a part of her knew that no one could make such promises. But for now, she was content to focus on the present, on the joy of baking with her family, and on the love that surrounded her.

Christmas Day was a celebration of family and love. The house was filled with the smell of roasting turkey, the sounds of Christmas music, and the laughter of children playing with their new toys. Karen watched with pride as Justin and Greg played with their children, passing on the traditions and values that she had instilled in them.

As the day drew to a close, the family gathered around the tree, exchanging gifts and sharing stories of Christmases past. Karen, sitting in her favorite chair with Jack in her lap, felt a deep sense of contentment. This was what she had fought for—the love, the laughter, the memories. As she looked around at her family, she knew that no matter what the future held, she would face it with courage and love.

In the quiet moments after the gifts had been exchanged and the children had been put to bed, Karen and Bradley sat together by the fire, their hands entwined.

"This was a perfect Christmas," Karen said softly, her voice filled with gratitude.

"It was," Bradley agreed, his eyes full of love as he looked at her. "And it's because of you, Karen. You make everything special."

Karen smiled, leaning into him. "We make everything special, Bradley. Together."

As they sat there, watching the fire crackle and dance, Karen felt a sense of peace settle over her. The future was uncertain, and she knew that there were still many challenges ahead. But she also knew that she had everything she needed to face those challenges—love, family, and the strength that came from knowing she was never alone.

As the snow fell softly outside, covering the world in a blanket of white, Karen made a silent promise to herself: to cherish every moment, to create as many memories as possible, and to continue fighting for the life and the love that meant everything to her.

Chapter 7
The Unseen Battles

The early months of 2018 brought with them a new rhythm for Karen and her family. With two grandchildren now a part of their lives, the focus had shifted to the joy of nurturing these new generations. However, the battle with cancer remained an ever-present reality, lurking in the background even during the happiest moments.

Karen's chemotherapy sessions continued, each one a grueling test of her physical and emotional endurance. The side effects had become a familiar if unwelcome, companion—nausea, fatigue, and neuropathy were constant reminders of the battle her body was fighting. Despite these challenges, Karen remained determined to be as present as possible for her family.

The spring of 2018 was unusually cold in Newfoundland, with lingering snow and frosty mornings that seemed reluctant to give way to the warmth of the season. But even as the weather dragged its feet, Karen found solace in the minor signs of life returning to her garden. The first buds appeared on the trees, and the crocuses began to push through the remaining snow, their delicate blooms a promise of the brighter days ahead.

Karen spent as much time outside as she could, wrapped in warm blankets, sitting in her garden. The fresh air and the sights and sound of nature were a balm to her soul, helping her to focus on the beauty around her rather than the pain and fatigue that had become such a part of her daily life.

Bradley continued to be her rock, his unwavering support a constant source of strength. He had taken on more responsibilities around the house, ensuring that Karen had everything she needed while also managing the renovations they had started the previous year. The bedrooms for the grandchildren—one for the boys and one for the girls—were nearly complete, each room a labor of love designed with Karen's input.

One afternoon, as Karen sat in the garden, Bradley joined her with a cup of tea. He handed it to her before settling down beside her, his presence warm and comforting.

"How are you feeling today?" Bradley asked, his voice soft and concerned.

Karen took a sip of the tea, letting the warmth spread through her. "Tired," she admitted, her voice tinged with fatigue. "But being out here helps. It reminds me that there's still so much beauty in the world."

Bradley nodded, reaching over to take her hand in his. "You've created so much beauty, Karen. In this garden, in our home, in our family. You've given us all so much."

Karen smiled, squeezing his hand gently. "I've tried, Bradley. I've tried to make the most of every moment."

"You've done more than try," Bradley said firmly. "You've succeeded. And we're all better for it."

They sat in companionable silence for a while, the sounds of birds chirping and the gentle rustle of leaves filling the air. Karen's thoughts drifted to the future, to the things she still wanted to do, the memories she still wanted to create with her grandchildren.

"I want to teach them," Karen said suddenly, her voice breaking the silence.

Bradley turned to her, a question in his eyes. "Teach who?"

"Lucy, Jack, and the others when they come," Karen explained. "I want to teach them about the garden, about how to bake, about the little things that matter. I want them to know me, to remember me, even when I'm not here."

Where Love Grows

Bradley nodded; his eyes filled with understanding. "They will, Karen. They'll remember all of it. And they'll carry you with them in everything they do."

Bradley's grip on her hand tightened slightly. "They will know you, Karen. You're leaving a legacy that will last far beyond your time. And I'll make sure they remember you every day."

Karen's eyes filled with tears, her heart full of love and gratitude. "Thank you, Bradley," she whispered. "For everything."

As the weeks passed, Karen began planning how she would spend time with her grandchildren. She started simple — inviting Lucy and Jack over for short visits, where they would sit together in the garden, or she would show them how to mix ingredients for cookies. Even at their young ages, the children were curious and eager to learn, their bright eyes wide with wonder at the world around them.

One day, as Karen sat with Lucy in the kitchen, showing her how to measure flour for a batch of cookies, the little girl looked up at her grandmother with a somber expression.

"Nanny Ner, why do you get tired sometimes?" Lucy asked, her tiny voice filled with concern.

Karen paused, her heart aching at the innocent question. "Well, sweetheart, Nanny is sick, and sometimes that makes me very tired," she explained gently. "But I'm still here, and I love spending time with you, even if I can't do as much as I used to."

Lucy nodded solemnly; her little brow furrowed in concentration as she processed this information. "Does the garden make you feel good?" she asked, her voice full of hope.

Karen smiled; her eyes moist with emotion. "Yes, Lucy, it does. The garden always makes me feel better. And so does spending time with you."

The moment was bittersweet—Karen knew that Lucy was too young to fully understand what was happening. However, she also knew that these moments were precious, each one a gift to be cherished.

As spring turned into summer, Karen's health remained stable, though the effects of chemotherapy continued to take their toll. She found herself more easily fatigued, often needing to rest after even the simplest of activities. But she refused to let the illness define her life. She continued to spend time with her family, to bake, to garden, and to create memories with her grandchildren.

Where Love Grows

One day in early July, as Karen sat in the garden with Bradley, she felt a sudden, sharp pain in her abdomen. It was different from the usual discomfort she had grown accustomed to, more intense and persistent. She tried to push it aside, not wanting to alarm Bradley, but the pain only grew worse as the day went on.

By evening, the pain had become unbearable. Bradley, seeing the distress on Karen's face, insisted on taking her to the hospital. Karen, who had always been reluctant to make a fuss, finally agreed, knowing that something wasn't right.

At the hospital, the doctors ran a series of tests, and Karen was admitted for observation. The news that followed was devastating—the cancer had spread to her liver. Despite the chemotherapy, the disease had continued its relentless march through her body.

When Dr. Matthews delivered the news, Karen felt as though the ground had been pulled out from under her. She had known this was a possibility, but hearing it confirmed was a different matter entirely. The weight of the diagnosis pressed heavily on her, and though she had prepared herself for difficult news, nothing could prepare her for the finality of it.

"I'm sorry, Karen," Dr. Matthews said gently, his voice filled with compassion. "We'll need to discuss our next steps. A liver resection may be necessary, and we'll have to reassess your chemotherapy regimen."

Karen nodded numbly, her mind reeling from the news. The prospect of another surgery, more treatments, more pain—it was almost too much to bear. But as she looked over at Bradley, who sat beside her, his face pale and drawn, she knew that she had no choice but to keep fighting.

"Let's do whatever we need to," Karen said quietly, her voice steady despite the turmoil inside her. "I'm not ready to give up."

The days that followed were a blur of medical consultations, tests, and preparations for surgery. Karen tried to stay focused on the positive—the fact that she was still here, still fighting, still surrounded by the love of her family. But there were moments when the fear and uncertainty threatened to overwhelm her when she would find herself lying awake at night, staring at the ceiling, wondering how much more her body could take.

The surgery was scheduled for late July, and once again, Karen and Bradley made the journey to St. John's, where the procedure would take place. The drive was somber, the weight of what lay ahead hanging over them like a dark cloud.

When they arrived at the hospital, Karen was admitted and prepped for surgery. The routine was familiar by now—the sterile smell of the hospital, the coldness of the IV needle, the soft beeping of the machines that monitored her vital signs. But this time, the fear was different, more profound. Karen knew that this surgery was riskier than the last and that the stakes were higher.

As she lay on the gurney, waiting to be taken into the operating room, Bradley leaned over and kissed her forehead. "I'll be right here when you wake up," he said softly, his voice filled with love. "You're the strongest person I know, Karen. You're going to get through this."

Karen nodded; her throat tight with emotion. "I love you, Bradley," she whispered, her voice trembling. "Thank you for being here with me."

"Always," Bradley replied, his eyes shining with unshed tears. "I'm not going anywhere."

The surgery was long and complicated, and when Karen finally woke up in the recovery room, the first thing she felt was pain—a deep, throbbing ache in her abdomen that made it hard to breathe. But even through the fog of pain, she was aware of Bradley's presence beside her, his hand holding hers, his voice a comforting murmur in the background.

"Karen, you're awake," he said softly, his relief palpable. "The surgery went well. The doctors were able to remove the tumor from your liver."

Karen nodded weakly, too exhausted to speak. The pain was overwhelming, but so was the sense of relief that the surgery was over. She had made it through another battle, another test of her strength and resilience.

The recovery was slow and painful. The surgery had taken a toll on her body, leaving her weak and vulnerable. The first few days were the hardest — Karen was in constant pain, unable to move without assistance, and even the simplest tasks required an enormous effort. But Bradley was there every step of the way, caring for her with a tenderness that brought tears to her eyes.

"You're doing great, Karen," he would say, his voice full of quiet encouragement. "Just take it one day at a time."

As the days turned into weeks, Karen slowly began to regain her strength. The pain started to subside, replaced by a dull ache that was easier to manage. She was able to sit up in bed, take short walks around the hospital corridors, and eventually return home to Pasadena.

The journey home was bittersweet. Karen was relieved to be leaving the hospital, but she knew the battle was far from over. The cancer was still there, still a threat, and the road ahead remained uncertain. Yet, as she looked out the window at the familiar landscape—the fields and forests that had always been her sanctuary—she felt a renewed sense of determination.

Pasadena had always been a place of healing for her, and now, more than ever, she was ready to draw strength from the life she had built there, from the love of her family, and from the memories she had yet to make.

"I'm going to keep fighting," Karen said quietly, more to herself than to Bradley. "I'm not giving up."

Bradley reached over and took her hand, his grip firm and reassuring. "I know you will," he said softly. "And I'll be right here with you every step of the way."

When they arrived home, Karen was greeted by the comforting sight of her garden. The flowers were in full bloom, the strawberries ripe and ready to be picked. But the garden, once a source of endless joy, now felt like a reminder of everything she had fought to hold onto.

Over the following weeks, Karen continued to recover, though the process was slow and fraught with challenges. The fatigue lingered, making even the simplest tasks a struggle. But she refused to let the illness define her life. She spent time with her grandchildren, teaching them about the garden, baking cookies, and creating memories that she hoped would last a lifetime.

One afternoon, as she sat in the garden with Lucy and Jack, Karen felt a deep sense of peace. The sun was warm on her face, the scent of flowers filled the air, and the sound of the children's laughter was music to her ears. At that moment, she knew that no matter what the future held, she had everything she needed — love, family, and the strength to keep fighting.

As the days passed, Karen held onto that peace and determination, and she faced each new challenge with courage and grace.

Chapter 8
The Tides of Change

The latter half of 2023 brought both joy and sorrow into Karen's life. As she continued her battle against cancer, the cycles of treatment, recovery, and recurrence became an exhausting rhythm that tested her endurance. Despite the physical toll, Karen remained determined to live fully and to be present for her family.

By the time fall arrived, the landscape around Pasadena was awash in vibrant colors. The trees were a mix of fiery reds, oranges, and yellows, a stark contrast to the challenges Karen faced. The garden, now preparing for winter, still managed to bring her comfort, even as the days grew shorter and the chill in the air became more pronounced.

The summer had been a difficult one. After her liver resection, Karen faced an arduous recovery, the pain and fatigue often overwhelming. Despite the challenges, she had insisted on maintaining her role as the family matriarch, refusing to let her illness overshadow the joy of being with her grandchildren.

One bright spot in the midst of her struggles was the news that Renee was expecting again. The prospect of another grandchild brought a surge of hope and excitement into Karen's life, a reminder that even in the darkest times, life continued to find a way.

In August 2022, Karen welcomed her fourth grandchild, Amelia, into the world. The birth was a moment of pure joy for the entire family. Karen reveled in the opportunity to hold another new life in her arms. She found herself drawn to the innocence and simplicity of her grandchildren, their laughter and curiosity providing a much-needed respite from the harsh realities of her illness.

As autumn settled in, Karen's health began to deteriorate more rapidly. The cancer had spread to her lungs, making breathing difficult and leaving her increasingly fatigued. The once manageable symptoms now became more severe, and she found herself facing new challenges that tested her resolve.

In early November 2023, Karen began experiencing a persistent cough that worsened over time. Concerned, Bradley insisted that she see Dr. Matthews. The visit confirmed what Karen had feared—the cancer had spread to her lungs, and the situation was dire.

Where Love Grows

Dr. Matthews explained the options available, but the prognosis was grim. "We can try another round of chemotherapy, but it's unlikely to be as effective as before," he said, his voice gentle but honest. "There's also the possibility of targeted radiation to help manage the symptoms, but the disease has progressed significantly."

Karen listened quietly, the weight of the news settling heavily on her. She had known this moment was coming, but it didn't make it any easier to hear.

"What do you think, Karen?" Dr. Matthews asked, his gaze meeting hers.

Karen took a deep breath, her thoughts racing. "I want to keep fighting, but... I don't want to spend the rest of my time in a hospital," she said softly. "I want to be at home, with my family, for as long as I can."

Bradley, who had been sitting beside her, reached for her hand, his grip firm and reassuring. "Whatever you decide, Karen, I'm with you," he said, his voice full of love.

Karen nodded, grateful for his unwavering support. "Let's try the radiation," she said finally. "If it can help with the symptoms, then it's worth it."

The decision was made, and Karen began a course of targeted radiation to address the tumors in her lungs. The treatments were grueling, leaving her even more fatigued than before, but she remained determined to keep going.

Throughout it all, Karen's focus remained on her family. She continued to spend as much time as possible with her grandchildren, savoring the moments of joy and connection they brought into her life. The sound of their laughter, the feel of their tiny hands in hers, and the sight of their bright, curious faces were constant reminders of what she was fighting for.

These moments of love and joy were what gave her strength, keeping her spirit alive through the toughest days.

One day, as Karen sat in the living room with Lucy and Jack, she noticed how much they had grown. Lucy, now six years old, was full of questions about the world around her, while Jack, now five, was a bundle of energy, constantly on the move.

"Nanny Ner," Lucy asked, her voice full of curiosity, "why do you have to go to the doctor so much?"

Karen hesitated, unsure of how to explain her illness to such young children. "Well, Lucy," she began gently, "Nanny is sick, and the doctors are helping me feel better. But it's important that I take care of myself so I can keep spending time with you."

Lucy nodded, her little face serious as she considered Karen's words. "I don't want you to be sick, Nanny Ner," she said softly, her eyes filling with tears.

Karen's heart broke at the sight of her granddaughter's sadness, but she forced herself to stay strong. "I know, sweetheart," she said, pulling Lucy into a comforting hug. "But I'm doing everything I can to get better. And as long as I'm here with you, I'm happy."

Jack, sensing the seriousness of the conversation, climbed into Karen's lap and snuggled close. "Nanny Ner, we love you," he said simply, his small voice filled with sincerity.

Tears welled in Karen's eyes as she held her grandchildren close. "I love you too, Jack," she whispered, her voice thick with emotion. "More than you'll ever know."

As the days passed, Karen's health continued to decline. The radiation had helped to some extent, but the cancer was relentless, its grip tightening with each passing week. The fatigue became overwhelming, and Karen found herself spending more and more time in bed, her energy drained by the simplest of tasks.

Bradley, ever attentive, took on more responsibilities around the house, ensuring that Karen had everything she needed. He arranged for a home care nurse to visit regularly, helping with medications and providing support as Karen's condition worsened. Despite the toll it took on him, Bradley remained steadfast in his care for Karen, his love for her never wavering.

One evening, as they lay in bed together, Karen turned to Bradley, her voice weak but filled with determination. "Bradley, there's something I need to ask you."

Bradley looked at her, his expression full of concern. "Anything, Karen. You know that."

"When the time comes, I want to go to the palliative care unit," she said quietly. "I don't want to put you through the pain of watching me suffer at home. I want to make it easier for you and for all of us."

Bradley's eyes filled with tears, and he took her hand in his, his grip firm but gentle. "Karen, I'll support whatever decision you make," he said, his voice choked with emotion. "But I want you to know that I'm not going anywhere. I'll be with you every step of the way, whether it's here at home or at the palliative care unit. I love you, Karen, and nothing will change that."

Karen smiled weakly, her heart swelling with love for the man who had been her partner through all the highs and lows of life. "I know, Bradley," she whispered. "And I love you too. So much."

The decision was made, and as May 2024 turned into June, Karen's health continued to deteriorate. The cancer had spread further, making it increasingly difficult for her to breathe and leaving her in constant pain. Despite the best efforts of her medical team, the pain became extremely difficult to manage, and Karen found herself relying more and more on morphine to find relief.

In early June, just before her 21st of June passing, Karen was admitted to the palliative care unit. The decision, though difficult, brought a sense of peace to both Karen and Bradley. The unit was quiet and comfortable, a place where Karen could receive the care she needed while surrounded by the love and support of her family.

The first few days in the unit were a blur of pain management and quiet conversations with the medical staff. The nurses were compassionate and attentive, doing everything they could to make Karen comfortable. Bradley remained by her side, holding her hand through the difficult moments, his presence a constant source of comfort.

As Karen's final days approached, her family gathered around her, filling the small room with warmth and love. Justin, Renee, Greg, and Sheena all took turns sitting with Karen, sharing stories, laughter, and quiet moments of reflection. Lucy, Jack, Anna, and Amelia, too young to fully understand the gravity of the situation, brought light and joy into the room with their innocent smiles and playful antics.

One evening, as the family sat together, the soft glow of the fading summer sun casting a warm light over the room, Karen looked around at the faces of her loved ones, her heart full.

"This is all I ever wanted," Karen said softly, her voice weak but filled with emotion. "To be surrounded by my family, to know that I'm loved. I'm so grateful for each and every one of you."

Tears filled the eyes of those around her as they listened to Karen's words, the weight of the moment settling over them.

"We're grateful for you, Mom," Justin said, his voice thick with emotion. "You've given us everything. We love you so much."

Karen smiled, her eyes wet with tears. "I love you all too," she whispered. "More than words can say."

As the days passed, Karen's condition continued to worsen. The pain became more intense, and despite the best efforts of the medical team, it was clear that the end was near. The family spent as much time as possible with Karen, cherishing every moment, every word, every touch.

On the evening of June 21, 2024, with Bradley by her side and her family gathered

Chapter 9:
The Final Goodbye

On June 21, 2024, the day Karen's family had been dreading finally arrived. The room in the palliative care unit was filled with a heavy, reverent silence as her loved ones gathered around her bed, their faces etched with a mixture of sorrow, love, and gratitude. The once-vibrant woman who had fought so bravely against cancer for a decade now lay peacefully, her breaths shallow and labored, each one a reminder of the fragility of life.

Bradley sat closest to her, holding her hand gently in his, his thumb tracing small circles on her skin. His eyes, red-rimmed and glistening with unshed tears, never left her face. For years, he had been her rock, her unwavering support, and now, in these final moments, he struggled to find the words to express everything he felt.

Karen's sons, Justin and Greg, stood on either side of the bed, their faces a reflection of the deep bond they shared with their mother. Their wives, Renee and Sheena, stood behind them, offering silent comfort. The grandchildren—Lucy, Jack, Anna, and Amelia—played quietly in the corner of the room, their innocent laughter and whispers a poignant contrast to the solemnity that hung in the air.

Karen's breathing grew more labored, and the room seemed to hold its breath with her. Bradley leaned in closer, his voice trembling as he spoke softly to her.

"I love you, Karen," he whispered, his voice thick with emotion. "You've been the best thing that ever happened to me. Thank you for all the love and for our life together. I don't know how I'm going to do this without you, but I promise I'll keep going. I'll look after the boys and the grandchildren. We'll all remember you every single day."

Karen's lips moved slightly as if trying to respond, but the effort was too much. Instead, a single tear escaped the corner of her eye, a silent acknowledgment of his words.

Justin, his voice choked with emotion, leaned down to kiss his mother's forehead. "Mom, you've given us everything," he said, his voice breaking. "We're so lucky to have had you as our mother. I'll make sure Lucy and Anna remember you, that they know what a strong, loving woman you were."

Greg, struggling to hold back his tears, gently squeezed Karen's other hand. "You've been our strength, Mom," he said quietly. "You've shown us what it means to love, to fight, and never to give up. I'll make sure Jack and Amelia grow up knowing how amazing their Nanny Ner was."

The grandchildren, sensing the change in the room's atmosphere, came closer, their small faces filled with confusion and concern. Lucy, the oldest, reached out to touch Karen's hand, her young mind grasping that something was happening, though she couldn't fully understand it.

"Nanny Ner, we love you," Lucy said softly, her voice innocent and pure. "We'll take care of the garden, just like you showed us."

Karen's breath hitched slightly, a faint smile playing on her lips at her granddaughter's words. It was as if, even in these final moments, she drew strength from the love of her family, from the knowledge that they would carry her legacy forward.

The minutes stretched into hours, each one filled with the quiet presence of love and sorrow. The sun began to set outside, casting a warm, golden glow through the window, bathing the room in a soft light. It felt as if the world itself was saying goodbye, offering one last beautiful moment to the woman who had filled so many lives with light.

Bradley continued to hold Karen's hand, his thumb still moving in gentle circles, his heart breaking with each passing moment. He leaned in close, pressing his forehead against hers, and whispered the words that had been on his heart for so long.

"Please forgive me, Karen," he said, his voice barely audible. "I forgive you. Thank you for everything."

A peaceful stillness settled over Karen's features, her breath coming slower and slower until finally, it stopped. The room seemed to pause, the weight of the moment sinking in as the reality of Karen's passing washed over them.

Bradley stayed where he was, holding Karen close, his tears falling freely now. The rest of the family gathered around, their grief raw and palpable but also tempered by the deep love they had for the woman who had just left them.

After what felt like an eternity, Bradley finally pulled back, his face wet with tears, but his expression calm and resolute. He looked around at his family, taking in the sight of each one of them, and felt a deep sense of gratitude for the life they had shared, the memories they had created, and the love that would endure long after Karen's passing.

"Let's remember her as she was," Bradley said quietly, his voice steady despite the tears that continued to fall. "Strong, loving, and full of life. She gave us everything, and now it's our turn to carry her legacy forward."

The family nodded, their hearts heavy but united in their love for Karen. They stayed in the room a while longer, sharing stories, memories, and quiet moments of reflection. The grandchildren, sensing the need for comfort, climbed into their parents' laps, their innocent presence a reminder that life, even in the face of death, continues.

As the night wore on, the family finally began to make their way out of the room, each one taking a moment to say a final goodbye to Karen. Bradley was the last to leave, his hand lingering on hers for just a moment longer before he gently placed it on her chest and kissed her forehead one last time.

"Goodbye, my love," he whispered, his voice breaking. "I'll carry you with me, always."

With that, he turned and walked out of the room, joining his family in the hallway. Together, they left the palliative care unit, stepping out into the cool night air, the stars twinkling above them

Where Love Grows

like a thousand tiny reminders that Karen's love and light would continue to shine down on them, guiding them through the days and years to come.

Chapter 10
The Healing Begins

In the weeks following Karen's passing, the Williams family found themselves navigating the complex process of grief. Each day brought its own set of challenges, from the quiet moments when her absence was most felt to the overwhelming waves of sorrow that seemed to come out of nowhere.

Bradley, in particular, struggled to adjust to life without Karen. The house, once filled with the warmth of her presence, now felt unbearably empty. The rooms she had so lovingly tended — the kitchen where she had baked countless cookies, the living room where they had spent so many evenings together, and, of course, the garden — now served as constant reminders of her absence.

Despite his grief, Bradley knew that he couldn't retreat into himself. Karen had made him promise that he would continue to live and find joy in the life they had built together, even after she was gone. And so, he threw himself into the tasks that needed to be done — taking care of the house, spending time with his sons and their families, and, most importantly, tending to the garden that had been Karen's sanctuary.

Where Love Grows

The garden, in many ways, became Bradley's own sanctuary. Each morning, he would rise early and make his way outside, the cool morning air a balm to his aching heart. He spent hours tending to the plants, pulling weeds, watering the flowers, and ensuring that everything was just as Karen had wanted. It was his way of staying close to her, of honoring her memory, and of keeping a part of her alive.

The grandchildren, too, played a crucial role in the family's healing process. Lucy, Jack, Anna, and Amelia, though young, understood in their own way that Nanny Ner was no longer with them. They missed her dearly, but they also brought a sense of joy and lightness to the family that helped ease the pain.

One afternoon, as Bradley was working in the garden, Lucy came up to him, her small hand clutching a bouquet of wildflowers she had picked from the edge of the yard.

"Grandpa, can we plant these in the garden?" she asked, her voice full of hope.

Bradley looked down at his granddaughter, her bright eyes so full of innocence and love, and felt a lump form in his throat. "Of course, Lucy," he said, his voice gentle. "Nanny Ner would have loved that."

Together, they found a spot near the pergola where the flowers would get plenty of sunlight. Bradley helped Lucy dig a small hole, and together, they carefully planted the wildflowers, patting the soil down around them.

As they worked, Lucy looked up at her grandfather, a question in her eyes. "Grandpa, do you think Nanny Ner can see us? Do you think she knows what we're doing?"

Bradley smiled, his heart swelling with love for the little girl who had brought so much joy into Karen's life. "I think she can, Lucy," he said softly. "And I think she's very proud of you."

Lucy smiled, a look of contentment settling over her features as she continued to work. When they were finished, she stood up and admired their handiwork, her face beaming with pride.

"It's beautiful, Grandpa," she said, her voice full of satisfaction. "Just like Nanny Ner's garden."

Bradley nodded, feeling a sense of peace settle over him. "It is, Lucy," he agreed. "And you helped make it that way."

The simple act of planting the flowers together brought Bradley a sense of healing he hadn't expected. It reminded him that life, even in the face of loss, continued on and that the love and memories they had shared with Karen would always remain a part of them.

As the weeks turned into months, the Williams family continued to find ways to honor Karen's memory. They gathered together for holidays and birthdays, keeping alive the traditions she had cherished. Bradley ensured that every Christmas was as special as it had been when Karen was with them, filling the house with the smells of her favorite recipes and the warmth of family.

In the garden, the flowers bloomed brighter than ever, a testament to the care and love that Bradley and the rest of the family had poured into it. The grandchildren played among the flowers, their laughter filling the air and bringing a sense of joy and continuity that eased the pain of Karen's absence.

One day, as Bradley was sitting on the porch, watching the grandchildren play in the garden, Justin joined him, a thoughtful expression on his face.

"Dad," Justin began, his voice quiet, "I've been thinking a lot about Mom lately. About everything she taught us, everything she gave us. I want to make sure that we don't lose sight of that, that we keep her memory alive in everything we do."

Bradley nodded, his eyes still on the garden. "Your mother was the heart of this family," he said softly. "She gave us so much — love, strength, and a sense of what really matters in life. We'll keep her memory alive, Justin. In the way we live, in the way we love, and in the way we take care of each other."

Justin smiled with a look of contentment on his face. "I'm glad, Dad. I want Lucy and Anna to grow up knowing how amazing their grandmother was and how much she loved them."

"They will, Justin," Bradley assured him. "Because we'll make sure of it."

As the sun began to set, casting a warm, golden light over the garden, Bradley felt a deep sense of peace. The pain of Karen's loss would never entirely go away, but he knew they would be okay. They had each other, they had the memories they had created with Karen, and they had the love that would carry them through the days and years to come.

As the stars began to twinkle in the sky above, Bradley looked up, a small smile playing on his lips. He knew that Karen was up there, watching over them, her love and light guiding them, just as it always had.

Chapter 11
A Legacy of Love

As the months passed after Karen's passing, the Williams family gradually settled into a new normal. The pain of losing her was still there, an undercurrent touching every part of their lives, but it was now accompanied by a sense of acceptance and peace. Karen's memory remained a constant presence in their home, and her influence was felt in the small, everyday moments that made up their lives.

Bradley continued to find solace in the garden, where every bloom and every new shoot felt like a message from Karen. He often spent hours there, tending to the plants and reflecting on the life they had built together. The garden had always been Karen's sanctuary, a place where she could escape the worries of the world and find peace among the flowers. Now, it was Bradley's sanctuary, too—a place where he felt closest to her.

One sunny afternoon in late summer, Bradley decided it was time to begin sharing the stories of

Karen's life with the grandchildren in a more deliberate way. He wanted them to understand not just who their grandmother was but also the values she had lived by — the love, resilience, and dedication that had defined her.

He gathered the family in the garden, where the children could play while the adults sat together, sharing memories and stories. It was a beautiful day, the sky a brilliant blue, with just a few wispy clouds floating lazily above. The garden was in full bloom, a riot of colors and scents that filled the air with a sense of life and renewal.

"Let's start a new tradition," Bradley suggested, his voice carrying over the sound of the children's laughter. "I want us to gather here, in this garden that Karen loved so much, and share stories about her. I want the grandchildren to know who their Nanny Ner was, what she stood for, and how much she loved them."

Justin, Greg, Renee, and Sheena all nodded in agreement, their expressions warm as they listened to Bradley's words. The idea of sharing Karen's stories, of keeping her memory alive through the generations, resonated deeply with each of them.

Lucy, who was now seven, was the first to speak up. "Can I tell a story about Nanny Ner?" she asked, her bright eyes filled with enthusiasm.

Bradley smiled and nodded. "Of course, Lucy. What do you want to share?"

Lucy thought for a moment, then began. "I remember when Nanny Ner showed me how to bake cookies. She let me mix the dough and put the chocolate chips in, and she told me that the secret ingredient was love. She said that's what made her cookies taste so good."

The adults smiled at the memory, and Bradley's heart swelled with pride. "That's right, Lucy," he said softly. "Your Nanny put love into everything she did—whether it was baking cookies, taking care of the garden, or spending time with her family. That's something she wanted to pass on to all of us."

Jack, who was now six, chimed in next. "Nanny Ner told me that the garden was like a family. She said that if you take care of the flowers and plants, they'll grow strong and beautiful, just like people do when they're loved."

Bradley nodded, his eyes moist with emotion. "She was right, Jack. And she took care of all of us, just like she took care of the garden. She made sure we were loved and that we had everything we needed to grow."

As the afternoon went on, each family member shared their own memories of Karen—stories of her kindness, her strength, and her unwavering love for her family. They laughed, cried, and found comfort in the knowledge that, even though Karen was no longer with them, her spirit lived on in the lives she had touched.

The tradition of gathering in the garden to share stories about Karen quickly became a cherished part of the Williams family's routine. Every few weeks, they would come together, the children excited to hear new tales about their grandmother while the adults found solace in the act of remembering.

As the seasons changed and the garden began to prepare for winter, Bradley made a decision. He wanted to create something permanent in the garden, a lasting tribute to Karen's life and legacy. After discussing it with Justin and Greg, they decided to build a small memorial near the pergola, where Karen had spent so many happy hours.

The memorial would be simple but meaningful—a stone bench engraved with Karen's name and a quote that had always been close to her heart: *"Love grows here."* It was a phrase that perfectly captured the essence of who Karen was and the way she had lived her life.

In early October, the family gathered once again in the garden, this time to unveil the memorial. The air was crisp, with the first hints of autumn in the breeze, and the leaves were beginning to turn. The garden, though past its peak bloom, was still a place of beauty and peace.

As the cover was lifted from the bench, there was a collective intake of breath. The bench was simple but elegant, the words "Love grows here" carved into the stone, a fitting tribute to the woman who had poured so much love into her family and her garden.

Bradley took a deep breath, his voice steady as he addressed his family. "This garden was Karen's sanctuary, a place where she found peace and joy. This bench is here to remind us of the love she planted in all of our hearts, the love that will continue to grow and flourish, just like the flowers in this garden."

The family sat on the bench, one by one, taking a moment to reflect on Karen's life and the impact she had on each of them. The children, too, understood the significance of the moment, their young minds grasping the idea that their grandmother's love would always be a part of them.

As they sat together, the sun began to set, casting a warm, golden light over the garden. It was a beautiful, peaceful moment, one that felt like a gift from Karen herself—a reminder that, even in her absence, she was still with them, watching over them, guiding them with her love.

The years would pass, and the garden would continue to bloom, a living testament to Karen's life and the legacy of love she had left behind. The bench became a place where the family would come to sit, to reflect, and to remember—a place where love truly did grow.

As the Williams family moved forward, they carried Karen's lessons with them, her love woven into the fabric of their lives, a constant presence that would guide them through whatever challenges and joys the future might bring.

Chapter 12
A New Generation

As the years continued to pass, the Williams family grew and changed. However, Karen's memory remains a constant presence in their lives. The garden, with its memorial bench and vibrant blooms, became a central gathering place for the family—a place where they could feel close to Karen and remember the love she had so generously shared.

By 2026, Lucy and Jack were eight years old, and Anna and Amelia were six and four, respectively. The children were growing up quickly, their personalities blossoming, each one showing traits that reminded the family of Karen. Lucy was kind and nurturing, always looking out for her younger siblings and cousins, much like Karen had cared for her own family. Jack was adventurous and curious, with a love for the outdoors that often led him to explore every corner of the garden. Anna was thoughtful and creative, frequently found drawing or writing stories about the garden and the family. And

Amelia, the youngest, was full of energy and laughter, her spirit bringing joy to everyone around her.

The garden, which had once been Karen's sanctuary, had now become a playground and a place of learning for the grandchildren. Bradley, who had taken on the role of caretaker for both the garden and the family, often found himself surrounded by the children, teaching them about the plants and flowers that Karen had loved so much.

One summer afternoon, as the family gathered in the garden, Bradley decided it was time to share more of Karen's wisdom with the grandchildren. He gathered them around the memorial bench, their eager faces turned up toward him, ready to listen.

"Do you know what this garden really is?" Bradley asked, his voice gentle.

Lucy, ever the thoughtful one, answered first. "It's Nanny Ner's garden. It's where she grew all the flowers and plants she loved."

Bradley smiled and nodded. "Yes, that's true, Lucy. But it's more than just a garden. It's a place where love grows. Your Nanny Ner believed that love was like a garden—you have to care for it, nurture it, and watch it grow. And just like the flowers in this garden, love can blossom into something beautiful if you take care of it."

Jack's brow furrowed in concentration, asked, "How do we take care of love, Grandpa?"

Bradley's heart swelled with pride at the question. "You take care of love by being kind to each other, helping when someone needs it, and being patient and understanding. Just like how we water the plants and pull the weeds, we take care of love by doing things that make it grow stronger."

Anna, who had been quietly listening, spoke up next. "Is that why Nanny Ner was always so nice to everyone? Because she was taking care of love?"

Bradley nodded, his eyes moist with emotion. "Exactly, Anna. Your Nanny Ner was one of the kindest, most loving people I've ever known. She took care of all of us, and that's why our family is so strong today. She planted seeds of love in each of our hearts, and it's up to us to keep those seeds growing."

Amelia, who had been playing with a small flower she had picked, looked up and asked, "Can we help the garden grow, too?"

Bradley smiled, reaching out to gently tuck a strand of Amelia's hair behind her ear. "Yes,

Amelia, you can. And by helping the garden grow, you're also helping to keep Nanny Ner's love alive."

The children were quiet for a moment, each of them absorbing Bradley's words. It was clear to Bradley that, even at their young ages, they understood the importance of what he was telling them. Karen's legacy was not just in the garden but in the way her love had shaped their family.

As the sun began to set, casting a warm, golden light over the garden, the family gathered together for a picnic dinner. The children ran and played among the flowers, their laughter filling the air. At the same time, the adults sat together, talking and reminiscing about Karen.

Renee, her eyes following Lucy as she helped Anna pick flowers, turned to Bradley and said, "Karen would be so proud of how you've kept the garden going and how you've taught the children to love it as much as she did."

Bradley smiled, though his heart ached with the familiar longing for his late wife. "I hope so, Renee. I like to think she's watching over us, seeing how the family is growing, and knowing that her love is still in all of us."

Greg, who was sitting beside his father, added, "You've done an incredible job, Dad. The garden is more than just a place to remember

Where Love Grows

Mom — it's become the heart of our family. Every time we're here, it feels like she's with us."

Bradley nodded, his throat tight with emotion. "That's all I ever wanted — to make sure that Karen's love would continue to be felt, even after she was gone."

The evening continued, the family sharing stories, laughter, and the simple joy of being together. As the stars began to appear in the sky, Bradley looked around at the faces of his children and grandchildren, and he felt a deep sense of peace.

The garden had always been a place of love and healing, and now it was a place of growth and learning, a living testament to Karen's life and the love she had planted in each of their hearts. Bradley knew that as long as the garden continued to bloom, so too would Karen's love, a guiding light for the generations to come.

As the night drew to a close and the family began to pack up, Lucy approached Bradley, her small hand slipping into his. "Grandpa, do you think I could take care of the garden with you? Like how Nanny Ner used to?"

Bradley looked down at his granddaughter, his heart swelling with pride and love. "I would love that, Lucy," he said, his voice warm. "We can take care of it together, just like Nanny Ner would have wanted."

And so, with Lucy by his side, Bradley continued to nurture the garden, teaching his grandchildren the lessons that Karen had taught him. The garden flourished under their care, a beautiful, living reminder of the love that had always been at the heart of their family.

The years would continue to pass, and the Williams family would grow and change, but the garden would remain—a place where love grew, where memories were cherished, and where Karen's legacy lived on in the hearts of those who loved her.

*****

This chapter focuses on the new generation of the Williams family, particularly the grandchildren, and how they begin to learn about and embrace the values that Karen lived by. The garden continues to serve as a central symbol of love and legacy, with Bradley passing on Karen's wisdom to the children. The chapter emphasizes the ongoing growth of the family and the ways in which Karen's memory and teachings continue to shape their lives.

~~~~~THE END~~~~~

Manufactured by Amazon.ca
Bolton, ON